WHEN I GROW UP
ABRAHAM LINCOLN

BY AnnMarie Anderson

ILLUSTRATED BY Gerald Kelley

Scholastic Inc.

"The best thing about the future is that it comes one day at a time."

— ABRAHAM LINCOLN

PHOTO CREDITS ©: cover: Anthony Berger/Brady's National Photographic Portrait Galleries/Library of Congress; cover background: StillFx/Thinkstock; 1 background: Jessica Meltzer; 3: Don Smetzer/Alamy Images; 4: Zeljko Radojko/Thinkstock; 6: Wislander/iStockphoto; 8: Paula Stephens/Thinkstock; 9: Hemera Technologies/ Thinkstock; 10 top left: Thinkstock; 10 top center: Steven Wynn/Thinkstock; 10 top right: Steven Wynn/Thinkstock; 13: George Barnard/Library of Congress; 16: Andrew_ Howe/iStockphoto; 18: Nikolay Mikheev/Thinkstock; 19: Valmol48/iStockphoto; 21 top, 22 top: Matthew B. Brady/Brady's National Photographic Portrait Galleries, 1865/Library of Congress; 22 bottom right, 22 bottom left: Matthew B. Brady/Brady's National Photographic Portrait Galleries/Library of Congress; 24: Library of Congress, Geography and Map Division; 25 top: Samuel Montague Fassett/Library of Congress; 25 bottom: iStockphoto; 26-27 background: Fort Sumter National Monument/National Park Service; 26: Ernest Crehen/Library of Congress; 28: The Strobridge Lith. Co., c1888/Library of Congress; 30: Library of Congress Rare Book and Special Collections Division; 31 top left: gwmullis/iStockphoto; 31 top right: Don Smetzer/Alamy Images; 31 center right: ermingut/iStockphoto; 31 bottom right: Vasiliki Varvaki/iStockphoto.

This unauthorized biography was carefully researched to make sure it's accurate. Although the book is written to sound like Abraham Lincoln is speaking to the reader, these are not his actual statements.

ISBN 978-0-545-60979-1

12 11 10 9 8 7 6 5 4 3 2   15 16 17 18 19 20/0
Printed in the U.S.A.   40
First printing, January 2015

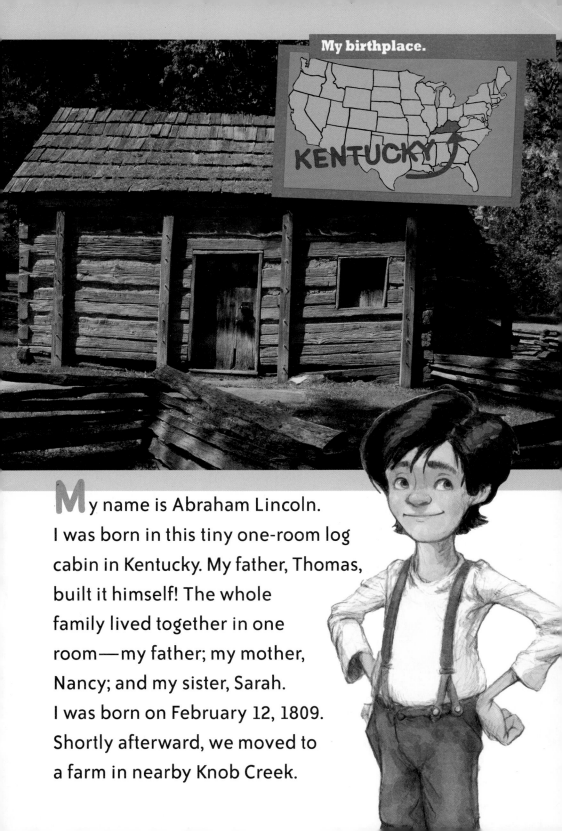

My birthplace.

KENTUCKY

My name is Abraham Lincoln. I was born in this tiny one-room log cabin in Kentucky. My father, Thomas, built it himself! The whole family lived together in one room—my father; my mother, Nancy; and my sister, Sarah. I was born on February 12, 1809. Shortly afterward, we moved to a farm in nearby Knob Creek.

My family didn't have much, but it was enough. My sister and I helped out on the farm. We carried water and wood for our mother. I helped my father plant corn and pumpkin seeds.

Sometimes I went fishing after my chores were done. One day I caught a big fish. I was excited to bring it home to my family for dinner. On my way home, I passed a tired and hungry soldier. My parents had taught me to be kind to others. The soldier looked like he needed a good meal, so I gave him my fish. It felt good. It felt like the right thing to do.

When I was six, a school opened nearby. My parents couldn't read and write much, but they wanted Sarah and me to learn. I learned the alphabet and a few words and numbers before the school closed. I wish I could have stayed at school. There was so much more to learn! But it was spring, and there was farmwork to do.

A one-room schoolhouse.

Just before I turned eight, my family moved to
a town called Little Pigeon Creek in Indiana. Our
land was covered in trees. My father and I had to
chop them down to make room for our new house.
From that time until I left home as a young man,
I almost always had an ax in my hands.

Soon after that, my mother got sick and died. The next year was a hard one. My father, sister, and I were very sad.

My father traveled to Kentucky and returned with a big surprise—a stepmother, two stepsisters, and a stepbrother! It was a big change, but it was good for all of us.

My stepmother, Sarah Bush Johnston, was warm and kind. She brought a lot of interesting books with her, including *Robinson Crusoe*, *Pilgrim's Progress*, and *Aesop's Fables*.

My father didn't value reading. He thought farmwork was more important. Luckily, my stepmother encouraged me to keep at it. I read her books and borrowed others. I loved reading about American history. I admired great American leaders like George Washington, Benjamin Franklin, and Thomas Jefferson. Sometimes I even read while I did my chores!

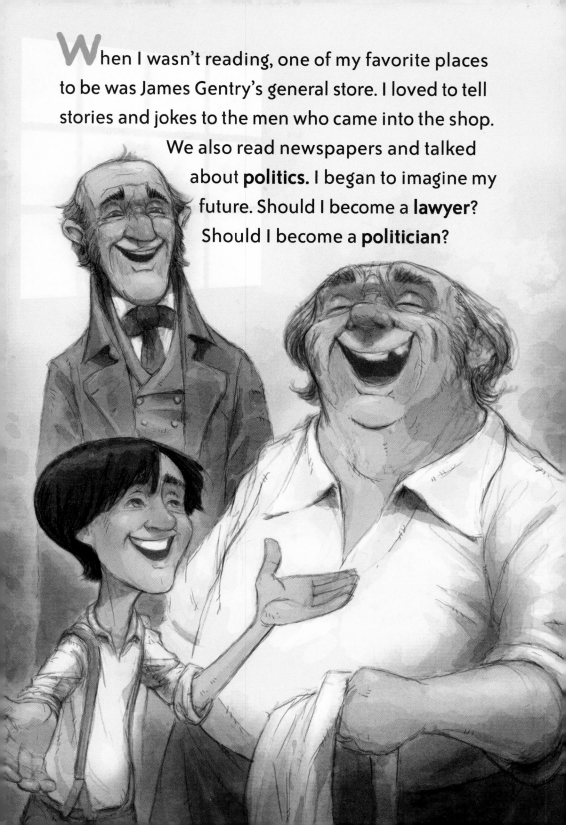

When I wasn't reading, one of my favorite places to be was James Gentry's general store. I loved to tell stories and jokes to the men who came into the shop. We also read newspapers and talked about **politics.** I began to imagine my future. Should I become a **lawyer**? Should I become a **politician**?

When I was nineteen, James Gentry offered me a job. His son Allen and I were hired to bring food and livestock down to New Orleans to be sold. We built a flatboat, filled it with corn, flour, potatoes, and bacon, and rowed it down the Ohio and Mississippi Rivers to New Orleans. It was a great adventure. New Orleans was incredible! I had never visited such a big city.

On my second trip to New Orleans, I saw a slave market. I hated it. Black people—men, women, and children—were captured, put in chains, and sold to **plantation** owners, who needed workers. Enslaved people didn't get paid and they had no rights! I knew slavery was wrong and unfair.

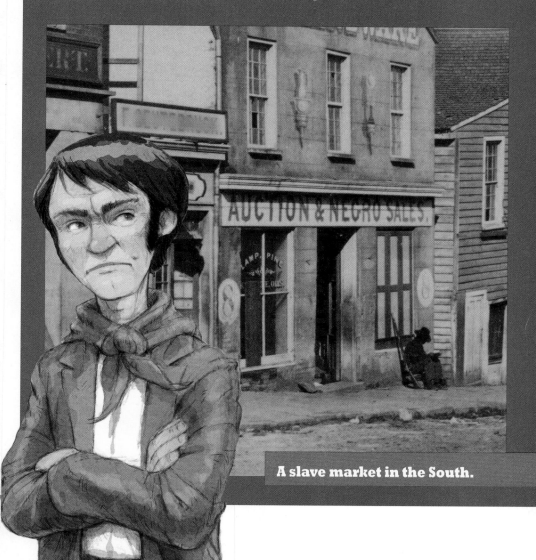

A slave market in the South.

Soon after I returned to Indiana, our family moved again, this time to Illinois. I helped my father build a new cabin there, but I was tired of farm life. When I was offered a job as a store clerk in the town of New Salem, Illinois, I said yes.

ILLINOIS

I was twenty-two years old when I said good-bye to my parents and left home. It was time for me to find my own way in the world.

I liked New Salem. As the store clerk, I had free time for reading poetry and plays and telling stories to customers. I made friends quickly. In the evenings, I studied history, grammar, and law. I joined the **debating** society. I learned how to express my thoughts using powerful words that made people think.

One day, a woman came into the store to buy some tea. After she had paid and left, I realized I had charged her too much. I walked all the way to her farm just to pay her back. Because of this and other examples, I earned the nickname "Honest Abe." I preferred to be called Abraham, but the nickname stuck.

The store closed, but I stayed in New Salem. Some friends encouraged me to run for the state **legislature**. If I won, I would represent the entire **county**. In the end, I lost the election, but many people voted for me. If I tried again, maybe next time I would win.

Fellow Citizens, I presume you all know who I am—I am humble Abraham Lincoln. I have been solicited by many friends to become a candidate for the legislature. My politics are short and sweet, like the old woman's dance. I am in favor of a national bank. I am in favor of the internal improvement system and a high protective tariff. These are my sentiments and political principles. If elected I shall be thankful; if not, it will be all the same.

I got a job as the town postmaster. I loved having the chance to read all the newspapers that were delivered with the mail. I also read books and taught myself how to work as a land **surveyor**. I continued meeting new people and making friends. When I was twenty-five, I ran for the state legislature again. This time I won!

I worked hard during my time in the Illinois legislature making laws to improve **transportation** and schools. I also prepared for my law exams. After three years of studying on my own, I passed the exams and became a lawyer.

I met a smart, charming woman named Mary Todd. In many ways, she was my opposite. I grew up poor and I was tall— 6 foot 4 inches! Mary's family was wealthy and she was more than a foot shorter than me. But we both liked books and politics. We got along well, and we were married in 1842.

Robert

Edward

William

Thomas

Mary and I lived in Springfield, Illinois, which was the state capital. In all, we had four sons— Robert, Edward, William, and Thomas. I loved my boys and played with them whenever I wasn't busy working. Sadly, two died young—Eddie died from **tuberculosis** at age four, and William died from **typhoid** at age eleven.

After serving in the Illinois state legislature for eight years, I was elected to **Congress** in 1846. I moved to Washington, D.C. My memory of seeing the slave market never left me. I made speeches against slavery, which had become a big issue that divided the country. States in the North wanted slavery to end. But states in the South used enslaved people to work on their farms. They felt they could not afford to lose them. My powerful speeches against slavery changed many people's minds.

After two years in Congress, I returned to Springfield. The fight over slavery continued to divide the North and the South. I was very worried about the country. But I continued to speak out against slavery. In 1860, people who agreed with me nominated me to run for president.

A map showing pro-slavery and antislavery states.

Antislavery States

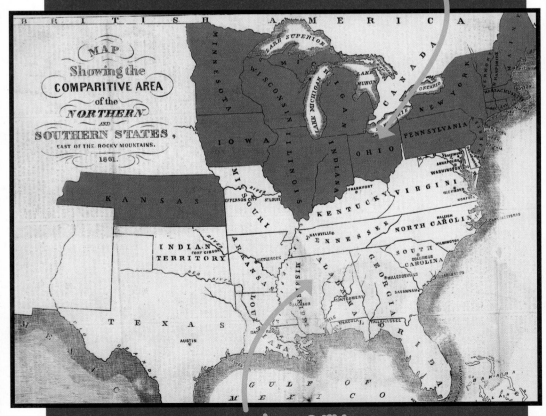

Pro-slavery States

Just before the election, I received a letter from an eleven-year-old girl from New York named Grace Bedell. She told me I would look better with "whiskers," and I took her advice. In 1861, I became the sixteenth president of the United States, and the first president with a beard.

Voters in the South were angry that I had been elected president. They knew I didn't support slavery. They feared I would **outlaw** it. So eleven southern states split, or **seceded**, from the United States of America. They formed their own country, the Confederate States of America. My worst fear had come true.

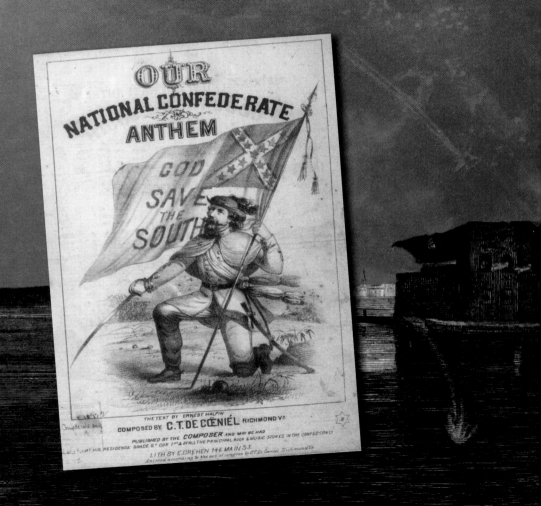

I was very unhappy. I wanted to keep the country united, not drive the North and South apart! But there was nothing I could do. And when Confederate soldiers attacked a United States fort in South Carolina, the country's long and painful **Civil War** began.

The attack on Fort Sumter.

The war dragged on and on. Many soldiers died on both sides. Families were torn apart. And slavery in the Confederate states continued. Then I wrote the Emancipation Proclamation. It said that all slaves in Confederate states were considered free as of January 1, 1863. Many enslaved people escaped to the North and joined the fight.

On July 4, 1863, there was a terrible battle in Gettysburg, Pennsylvania. More than fifty thousand soldiers died. A cemetery was built for all the soldiers who were killed. On November 19, I made a short speech at the cemetery, called the Gettysburg Address. I reminded the country how special our **democracy** was, and how important it was for the North and South to reunite. My speech that day inspired people to work to make our nation great. After four years of fighting, the Confederate states surrendered on April 9, 1865. The war was finally over!

To celebrate, Mary and I went out to see a play a few days later. But not everyone was happy that the North had won. A man named John Wilkes Booth was so angry that he snuck into the theater and shot me.

I died the next morning. The country was shocked and saddened. A funeral train draped in black banners carried me home to Springfield, Illinois. Along the way, millions of people watched the train pass by and said good-bye to their friend and president, Abraham Lincoln.

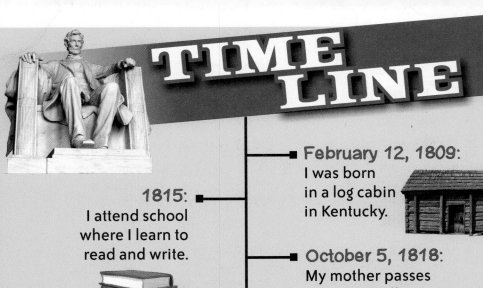

TIME LINE

February 12, 1809:
I was born in a log cabin in Kentucky.

1815:
I attend school where I learn to read and write.

October 5, 1818:
My mother passes away tragically.

March 1833:
I become the town postmaster.

1834:
I run for state legislature for a second time and win the election!

September 1836:
I pass legal exams and become a lawyer.

November 4, 1842:
I marry Mary Todd.

August 3, 1846:
I am elected to Congress.

1860:
I am nominated for and elected president.

1860–1861:
The Confederate states secede and the Civil War begins.

January 1, 1863:
I sign the Emancipation Proclamation declaring all citizens free.

April 9, 1865:
The Confederacy surrenders and the Civil War ends.

GLOSSARY

Civil War: A war fought in the United States from 1861–1865, between the Union in the North and the Confederacy in the South.

Congress: A governing body of the United States that makes laws.

county: A division or part of a state with its own local government.

debating: To argue a point from opposing sides.

democracy: A way of governing a country in which the people choose their leaders in elections.

lawyer: A person who is trained to advise people about the law.

legislature: A group of people who have the power to make or change laws for a country or a state.

plantation: A large farm where crops such as coffee, tea, and cotton are grown.

politician: Someone who runs for or holds government office.

politics: The debate and activity involved in governing a country.

secede: Withdraw formally from a group or organization.

surveyor: Someone who measures an area in order to make a map or plan.

transportation: A means or system for moving people and freight from one place to another.

tuberculosis: A highly contagious bacterial disease that usually affects the lungs.

typhoid: A serious infectious disease that is caused by germs in water or food.